A Guide to
AMERICAN STATES

California

THE GOLDEN STATE

MEDIA ENHANCED BOOKS
AV2 BY WEIGL
ADDED VALUE • AUDIO VISUAL

www.av2books.com

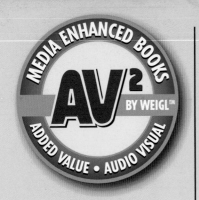

AV² provides enriched content that supplements and complements this book. Weigl's AV² books strive to create inspired learning and engage young minds in a total learning experience.

Your AV² Media Enhanced books come alive with...

Audio
Listen to sections of the book read aloud.

Key Words
Study vocabulary, and complete a matching word activity.

Go to **www.av2books.com**, and enter this book's unique code.

Video
Watch informative video clips.

Quizzes
Test your knowledge.

BOOK CODE

K 4 0 6 1 0 0

Embedded Weblinks
Gain additional information for research.

Slide Show
View images and captions, and prepare a presentation.

AV² by Weigl brings you media enhanced books that support active learning.

Try This!
Complete activities and hands-on experiments.

... and much, much more!

Published by AV² by Weigl
350 5th Avenue, 59th Floor
New York, NY 10118
Website: www.av2books.com   www.weigl.com

Library of Congress Cataloging-in-Publication Data

Parker, Janice.
 California / Janice Parker.
   p. cm. -- (A guide to American states)
 ISBN 978-1-61690-777-8 (hardcover : alk. paper) -- ISBN 978-1-61690-452-4 (online)
 1. California--Juvenile literature. I. Title.
 F861.3.P375 2011
 979.4--dc22
                         2011018316

Printed in the United States of America in North Mankato, Minnesota

052011
WEP180511

Project Coordinator Jordan McGill
Art Director Terry Paulhus

Photo Credits
Every reasonable effort has been made to trace ownership and to obtain permission to reprint copyright material. The publishers would be pleased to have any errors or omissions brought to their attention so that they may be corrected in subsequent printings.

Weigl acknowledges Getty Images as its primary image supplier for this title.

Contents

The Hollywood Sign, located in Griffith Park, was bulit in 1923.

Introduction

California's warm climate, beautiful landscapes, exciting attractions, and economic opportunities have long drawn people from around the world. California has by far the most residents of any U.S. state, with more than 37 million people, and it is the third-largest state in area. Beautiful beaches, rocky cliffs, snowy mountains, barren deserts, and lush forests are all within close distance from one another. There are several theories about the origin of the state's name, but many people think it came from a Spanish novel written in the 1500s. The book described an fictional island east of Asia called California.

Giant California Redwoods can be found along California's northern coast.

Visitors from all over the world come to enjoy California's scenic beaches.

California is well known for its entertainment industry. Many of the world's motion pictures and television programs are created and shot in the state. The center of the movie and TV industry is Hollywood, a district within Los Angeles. Movie stars can be seen walking down the street in some California cities. People from all over North America and the world move to California with dreams of becoming successful in show business. People also come to California for many other reasons. Many come as visitors to see California's tourist destinations, such as Disneyland, located in Anaheim. Some move to the state simply because they love the warm climate and the way of life. California is home to many people who enjoy active lifestyles and healthy food. The abundance of farms in the state makes it easy to eat fresh, locally grown fruits and vegetables.

Where Is California?

California is located on the west coast of the United States. There are many different ways to reach the state. Major airports are located in Los Angeles, San Diego, San Jose, San Francisco, and Oakland. These and the state's many other airports carry passengers within the state and to destinations across the country and around the world.

Los Angeles International Airport, or LAX, is the sixth busiest airport in the world.

Train travelers can arrive on various rail lines that end up in large cities including Los Angeles and San Francisco. Passenger trains stop in most major California cities. Automobile travel is very common in the state, and the many freeways and other highways make nearly all parts of California reachable by car.

Since the gold rush brought many people to the state in the mid-1800s, California's population has grown dramatically. The state's large population is made up of **diverse** cultural and ethnic groups. Hispanic culture has made a significant impact throughout California. Many of the state's cities and physical features bear Spanish names. In the 20th and 21st centuries, Hispanic American immigrants and their descendants, particularly Mexican Americans and people who trace their origins to Central America, have had a great influence. Immigrants from other parts of the world, particularly Asia, have also left their imprint on California.

San Francisco's Chinatown is a popular tourist destination.

Mapping California

C alifornia is bordered by Nevada and Arizona to the east, Oregon to the north, and Mexico to the south. The western border is defined by the Pacific Ocean. California has the second-longest coastline in the **contiguous** United States, after Florida. Its coastline is 840 miles long.

Sites and Symbols

STATE SEAL
California

STATE BIRD
California Quail

STATE FLOWER
California Poppy

STATE FLAG
California

STATE GEMSTONE
Benitoite

STATE TREE
California Redwood

Nickname The Golden State

Motto *Eureka* (I Have Found It)

Song "I Love You, California" words by F. B. Silverwood and music by Alfred Frankenstein

Entered the Union September 9, 1850, as the 31st state

Capital Sacramento

Population (2010 Census) 37,253,956 Ranked 1st state

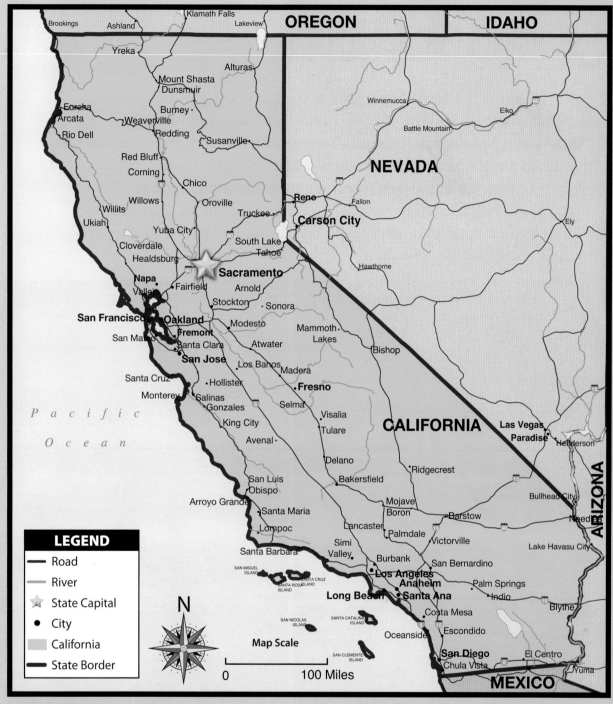

Map labels:

OREGON · IDAHO · NEVADA · CALIFORNIA · ARIZONA · MEXICO

Brookings · Ashland · Klamath Falls · Lakeview · Yreka · Alturas · Mount Shasta · Dunsmuir · Burney · Eureka · Arcata · Weaverville · Redding · Susanville · Rio Dell · Red Bluff · Corning · Chico · Oroville · Willows · Willits · Ukiah · Yuba City · Truckee · Cloverdale · South Lake Tahoe · Healdsburg · Sacramento · Napa · Vallejo · Fairfield · Arnold · Stockton · Sonora · San Francisco · Oakland · Modesto · Fremont · Santa Clara · Atwater · Mammoth Lakes · San Jose · Los Banos · Madera · Bishop · Santa Cruz · Fresno · Hollister · Monterey · Salinas · Selma · Gonzales · Visalia · King City · Tulare · Avenal · Delano · Bakersfield · Ridgecrest · San Luis Obispo · Arroyo Grande · Mojave · Boron · Barstow · Santa Maria · Lancaster · Palmdale · Victorville · Lompoc · Simi Valley · Burbank · San Bernardino · Santa Barbara · Los Angeles · Anaheim · Palm Springs · Long Beach · Santa Ana · Indio · Costa Mesa · Blythe · Oceanside · Escondido · San Diego · El Centro · Chula Vista · Yuma

Winnemucca · Elko · Battle Mountain · Reno · Fallon · Ely · Carson City · Hawthorne · Las Vegas · Paradise · Henderson · Bullhead City · Needles · Lake Havasu City

Pacific Ocean

SAN MIGUEL ISLAND · SANTA CRUZ ISLAND · SANTA ROSA ISLAND · SAN NICOLAS ISLAND · SANTA CATALINA ISLAND · SAN CLEMENTE ISLAND

LEGEND

— Road
— River
⭐ State Capital
• City
▢ California
— State Border

N

Map Scale

0 — 100 Miles

STATE CAPITAL

Sacramento, with a population of 467,000, became California's state capital in 1854. Previous capitals were San Jose, Vallejo, and Benicia. Sacramento is in north-central California, about 70 miles northeast of San Francisco Bay.

United States

California

Hawai'i · Alaska

The Land

California is a land of contrasts. It contains both the highest and lowest points in the 48 contiguous U.S. states and includes fertile valleys, forests, sandy beaches, arid deserts, and extensive mountain ranges. Much of the eastern part of the state is a desert region. To the west of the desert region rise mountain ranges, such as the Sierra Nevada. Other major mountain ranges in the state are the Klamath Mountains, in northwestern California, and the southern part of the Cascade Range.

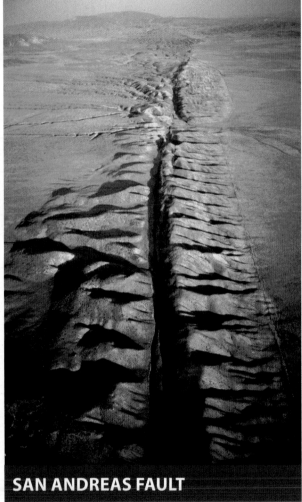

SAN ANDREAS FAULT

The San Andreas Fault is a fracture in Earth's surface that runs north-south through the state for more than 800 miles. Earthquakes often occur along this fault.

CENTRAL VALLEY

The great Central Valley, which runs 450 miles from north to south and covers about 18,000 square miles, is almost totally enclosed by mountains.

MOJAVE DESERT

California's largest desert, the Mojave, covers more than 25,000 square miles. It also spreads into Nevada, Arizona, and Utah.

MOUNT WHITNEY

The highest point in California is Mount Whitney. At 14,494 feet, it is also the highest point in the continental United States outside of Alaska.

I DIDN'T KNOW THAT!

Death Valley is 282 feet below sea level. It is the lowest point in California and the continental United States.

There are 18 national forests in California.

Mount Shasta is one of the active volcanoes in California. Others include Lassen Peak and Coso Peak.

Californians enjoy a lot of sunny and warm weather, especially in the southern part of the state.

Climate

With so many landscapes, California also has many different climates. Southern coastal areas are sunny and warm with mild winters. Northern coastal areas are also mild but cooler. The valley and foothill areas are hot and dry in the summer and cold and humid in the winter. Summers in the mountain areas are warm. The desert areas are very dry and hot.

The average temperature in California is about 44° Fahrenheit in January and about 75° F in July. Temperatures vary considerably, however. In Susanville, in mountainous northeastern California, the average temperature in January is 31° F, and in July it is 69° F.

Average Annual Precipitation Across California

California's annual precipitation averages about 22 inches a year, but the amount varies greatly by region. In general, rain falls mainly in the winter. Why might some areas of the state receive much more rainfall than others?

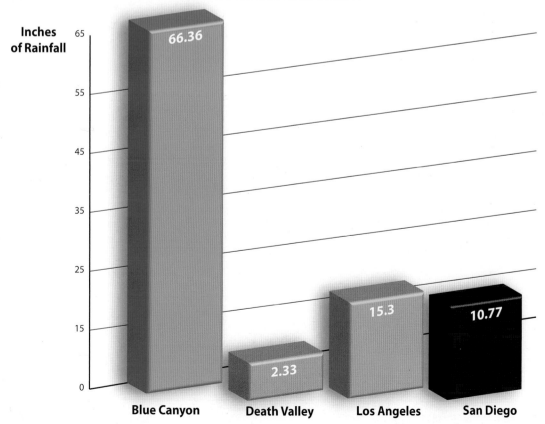

Natural Resources

Timber is an important natural resource in California. Almost 40 percent of the state is covered with forests. Among the most common trees are firs, pines, and oaks.

The state is rich in marine life such as crabs and tuna. Fish and shellfish, including lobsters and shrimp, are caught off the coast of California. Other economically important catches include sardines, salmon, rockfish, black cod, sole, swordfish, and urchin.

Because nearly half the state is forested, timber is one of California's most important resources.

California's minerals are another important resource. Cement, sand, gravel, and stone are mined in **quarries** and used throughout the United States. Water, including the Pacific Ocean, rivers, and lakes, is an important resource for agriculture and tourism. California's rivers help provide power through **hydroelectricity**.

California is one of the country's top five seafood-producing states.

California has about 43 million acres of farmland.

Minerals found in California include platinum, copper, and tungsten.

One huge sequoia has been cut to allow cars to pass through it.

California has more than 1,400 dams on its rivers to help control floods and store water for use in the long, dry summers or during droughts.

Plants

California's plant life is as varied as its geography and climate. Northern California has woodlands that contain some of the world's tallest trees, the coastal redwoods. Giant sequoia trees in the Sierra Nevada are the largest of all trees in bulk. Their trunks can sometimes measure up to 40 feet across. Other common trees are oak, aspen, palm, and eucalyptus. Common plants found in California are the flowering dogwood and myrtle. The desert areas contain many different species of **succulents**. The state flower, the golden poppy, grows in the Central Valley. Creosote and mesquite are some of the few plants that can survive in the hot, dry climate of Death Valley.

BRISTLECONE PINE TREE

These unusual-looking trees grow in the White Mountains. One bristlecone pine, nicknamed Methuselah, is thought to be more than 4,700 years old.

GOLDEN POPPY

The golden poppy was designated California's state flower in 1903. Residents celebrate April 6 as California Poppy Day.

JOSHUA TREE

The Joshua tree is the largest member of the yucca family. These trees can be found in the southeastern part of the state.

CALIFORNIA REDWOOD

Also known as the Coast Redwood, these massive trees can reach heights of more than 350 feet.

The Sierra Club is a national **conservation** group that was founded in California in 1892 by John Muir. Muir, an environmentalist, aimed to protect the mountain regions of the West coast. The Sierra Club now has branches in all 50 of the United States.

Creosote bushes found in the Mojave Desert can be as much as 11,500 years old.

Animals

California is home to many different types of animals. Marine animals, such as otters, seals, and whales, can be found off the coast. Coyotes, hares, and lizards roam in desert areas. Cougars, black bears, and bobcats live in the forests. Many different bird species spend all or part of the year in California. Seagulls, terns, and pelicans live along the coast. Spotted owls live in the northern forests.

The California condor, which can fly at speeds of up to 55 miles per hour, is an **endangered** species. It is one of the largest species of birds in the world. Though once there were hundreds throughout the state, human habitation disturbed and destroyed their **habitat**, and the condors began to die out. In 1982 there were only about 20 of the birds left. Conservation groups have tried to save the California condor by breeding birds in **captivity** and releasing them. Today there are about 160 California condors living in the wild. Several other California animals are endangered, including the riparian brush rabbit, the San Joaquin kit fox, and several species of kangaroo rats.

SEA LION

California is home to nearly 240,000 sea lions. Groups of these playful animals can be seen in many coastal areas.

DESERT COTTONTAIL

The desert cottontail is the most common rabbit found in California's deserts and valleys. Cottontails avoid extreme heat by resting in the shade on hot summer days.

BIGHORN SHEEP

The Sierra Nevada bighorn sheep was listed as an endangered species in California in 2000. The sheep usually live on rocky or grassy mountain slopes and are excellent climbers.

CALIFORNIA QUAIL

The state bird of California is known for the curved black crown feather on its forehead. This ground-dwelling bird adapts easily to different environments and can be found throughout the state.

The California grizzly bear is the state animal, but it has been extinct in California since 1922.

Each year thousands of swallows leave and return to the area around the San Juan Capistrano mission. Residents celebrate their departure in October and their return in mid-March.

Tourism

Tourism is an important industry in California, contributing more than $87 billion annually to the state's economy. The state's eight national parks are some of the most popular in the country. Los Angeles, San Francisco, and San Diego attract many visitors from elsewhere in the country and around the world. Families come to visit the state's many amusement parks and zoos.

Many people come to California for its coastline. People come to enjoy the beautiful beaches and sports such as surfing, windsurfing, and sailing. Visitors may drive along scenic Highway 1, which follows the shoreline for much of the way between San Francisco and Los Angeles. Along this drive is Big Sur, a 100-mile-long, ruggedly beautiful stretch of seacoast.

DISNEYLAND

Disneyland, which opened in 1955, was the first Disney theme park. It has had more than 600 million visitors since its opening.

HOLLYWOOD

Hollywood, in Los Angeles, is considered the center of the U.S. film industry. Visitors come to the area to take tours and see the homes of movie stars.

SAN DIEGO ZOO

Known for the care it takes to reproduce natural habitats, the San Diego Zoo is one of the most popular zoos in the world. It is home to more than 4,000 animals, including pandas.

GOLDEN GATE BRIDGE

The Golden Gate Bridge, completed in 1937, is one of San Francisco's most popular tourist attractions. It is estimated that 9 million people visit the bridge every year.

Alcatraz Island, located in San Francisco Bay, was formerly a federal prison that housed some of the country's most dangerous prisoners, including gangster Al Capone. The island is now a popular tourist attraction.

The Aquarium of the Pacific in Long Beach is home to more than 12,000 ocean creatures.

Hearst San Simeon State Historical Monument, once the estate of publisher William Randolph Hearst, attracts visitors from around the world. The vast main residence covers 60,000 square feet and contains 115 rooms.

Industry

Manufacturing, tourism, and agriculture are some of the leading industries in California. The entertainment industry provides jobs for many Californians. Actors, directors, screenwriters, camera operators, and special-effects staff all help to create films and television shows.

Industries in California
Value of Goods and Services in Millions of Dollars

California is known for its entertainment and technology industries, but the state's workers are employed in many different fields. Why might health care be such a large industry?

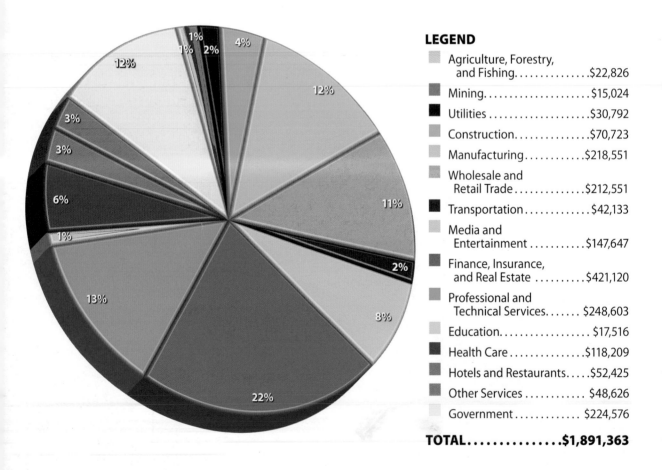

LEGEND

Agriculture, Forestry, and Fishing	$22,826
Mining	$15,024
Utilities	$30,792
Construction	$70,723
Manufacturing	$218,551
Wholesale and Retail Trade	$212,551
Transportation	$42,133
Media and Entertainment	$147,647
Finance, Insurance, and Real Estate	$421,120
Professional and Technical Services	$248,603
Education	$17,516
Health Care	$118,209
Hotels and Restaurants	$52,425
Other Services	$48,626
Government	$224,576
TOTAL	**$1,891,363**

Percentages may not add to 100 because of rounding.

Businessmen Levi Strauss and Jacob Davis received a patent for blue jeans in San Francisco in 1873. Levi's® is now one of the best-known brands of jeans in the world.

In 1939, William Hewlett and David Packard founded a company in Packard's garage in Palo Alto. The Hewlett-Packard Company would become the center of what is now Silicon Valley.

California is the country's leading agricultural state. More than 350 crops are commercially planted and harvested in the state.

Along the southern shores of San Francisco Bay is Silicon Valley, an industrial area famous for its high-technology industry. The nickname is derived from the material silicon, which is used to make microchips for computers and other electronic equipment. Many of the world's leading high technology companies were founded or have offices in Silicon Valley. Several companies design and manufacture microchips.

Google has offices throughout the world, but its headquarters are located in Silicon Valley.

Goods and Services

The service sector accounts for a large portion of the total value of goods and services in California. Service jobs are varied, including actors, social workers, government employees, doctors, schoolteachers, and bus drivers.

Agriculture is vital to the state's economy. California's more than 80,000 farms produce large quantities of nuts, fruits, and vegetables. Leading agricultural products include milk and grapes. America's almonds, pomegranates, walnuts, raisins, and olives come almost entirely from California. The state also produces more greenhouse and nursery products, such as potted plants and cut flowers, than any other state.

California residents can enjoy locally grown fruits and vegetables from the state's thousands of farms.

The gold rush is long over, but gold is still an important part of California's economy.

The counties of Sonoma and Napa are known for wine production. The region is home to more than four hundred wineries.

California produced many of the ships and aircraft used during World War II.

An ad campaign featuring California raisin animation figures became so popular during the 1980s that it was made into a television series. *California Raisins* was on the air in the 1989–1990 season.

California is a leading U.S. state for manufacturing. Factories make aircraft, ships, military supplies, electrical equipment, and chemicals. California also has many food processing plants and publishing and printing businesses.

California produces more gold than most other states, and gold mining has played an important role in the history of the state. Shortly after California became a U.S. territory, gold was discovered at Sutter's Mill, near the Sacramento River. In 1849 people in search of gold came to California from all over the world. The people were called "forty-niners." The gold rush ended almost as quickly as it had begun and was mostly over by 1854.

First Americans in the Arts, a non-profit organization that recognizes American Indian contributions to the entertainment industry, holds an annual festival in Los Angeles.

American Indians

Scientists believe that about 15,000 to 20,000 years ago, people crossed from what is now Siberia, in northern Asia, to North America by means of a land bridge that connected the two continents. That land bridge is now covered by the Bering Strait. Human beings then spread throughout North and South America, coming to occupy California probably by about 12,000 years ago. The prehistoric settlers in California were isolated from others on the continent by the high mountains. By the 1500s the area that is now California had the greatest concentration of American Indian peoples in North America.

The early American Indian groups in California included the Hupa, who lived in the far northwest. The Ohlone lived in the San Francisco area, and the Pomo to the north. The Maidu made their home in north-central California, and the Yuma, or Quechan, lived in the southernmost reaches. Some of the other native groups were the Cahuilla, Chumash, Karuk, Mojave, Yokuts, Paiute, and Modoc. The native peoples of California spoke many different languages and **dialects**. They usually lived together peacefully.

I DIDN'T KNOW THAT!

To overcome the scarcity of water, the Cahuilla dug wells to get water for cultivating vegetables and fruits.

Before European Americans arrived in California, there may have been as many as 300,000 American Indians. By 1900 there were only about 16,000. Many American Indians died of new diseases brought by the Europeans.

Native people in northern California made baskets for carrying food and infants. Those who lived near the coast used shells as money.

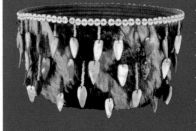

Cave paintings made by early native peoples can be seen in in the San Emigdio Mountains.

Explorers and Missionaries

On September 28, 1542, João Rodrigues Cabrilho, a Portuguese sailor, landed at San Diego Bay. He was the first European to reach what is now California. Cabrilho, who claimed the land for Spain, went on to explore the Catalina Islands and sailed farther north to view the area that is now Santa Monica and the Channel Islands. In 1579 the English explorer Sir Francis Drake traveled to the San Francisco area. Drake claimed the land for England.

Drake's visit encouraged the Spanish to return to the area. In the 1580s and 1590s Francisco Gali and Sebastian Rodriguez Cermeño sailed along the northern California coast, exploring Cape Mendocino and Monterey Bay. In 1602 Sebastian Vizcaíno sailed from Mexico to explore the coast of California. He reported his findings to the Spanish king, urging him to create a colony in the area. Not until 1769, however, did another Spanish **expedition** travel to California. The first Spanish mission in California was San Diego de Alcalá, which was built near San Diego in 1769. Over the next half century, 20 other missions were built from San Diego to Sonoma. The Spanish built military forts, called presidios, near many of the missions. The **missionaries** tried to get the American Indians to give up their own spiritual beliefs and adopt Christianity. Many American Indians resisted the beliefs and culture of the missionaries.

A statue in San Diego honors João Rodrigues Cabrilho.

Timeline of Settlement

Early Exploration

1542 Portuguese sailor João Rodrigues Cabrilho lands at San Diego Bay. He is the first European to reach what is now California. Cabrilho claims the land for Spain.

1579 Sir Francis Drake, an English explorer, travels to San Francisco. He claims the land, which he calls New Albion, for England.

1602 Sebastian Vizcaíno sails from Mexico to explore the coast of California.

First Settlements

1769 The first Spanish mission, San Diego de Alcalá, is built in California.

1781 The city of Los Angeles is founded by the Spanish.

1812 A group of Russian fur traders and fur trappers establishes Fort Ross as a base for hunting and trading.

Under Different Flags

1821 After eleven years of war, Mexico wins independence from Spain. Present-day California becomes part of Mexico.

1846 The Mexican-American War begins between the United States and Mexico.

1848 The Treaty of Guadalupe Hidalgo ends the Mexican-American War. Most of the Southwest, including California, is transferred from Mexico to the United States.

Gold and Statehood

1849 Hundreds of thousands of people flock to California after gold is discovered the year before. The gold was discovered at John Sutter's sawmill in Coloma.

1850 California becomes the 31st state on September 9th.

Early Settlers

I n 1812 a group of Russian fur traders moved south from Alaska to the northwest coast of California. They established Fort Ross, about 60 miles north of San Francisco, as a base for the hunting of seals and otters. Russian traders stayed until 1841, when they sold the fort to the American pioneer Captain John A. Sutter.

Map of Settlements and Resources in Early California

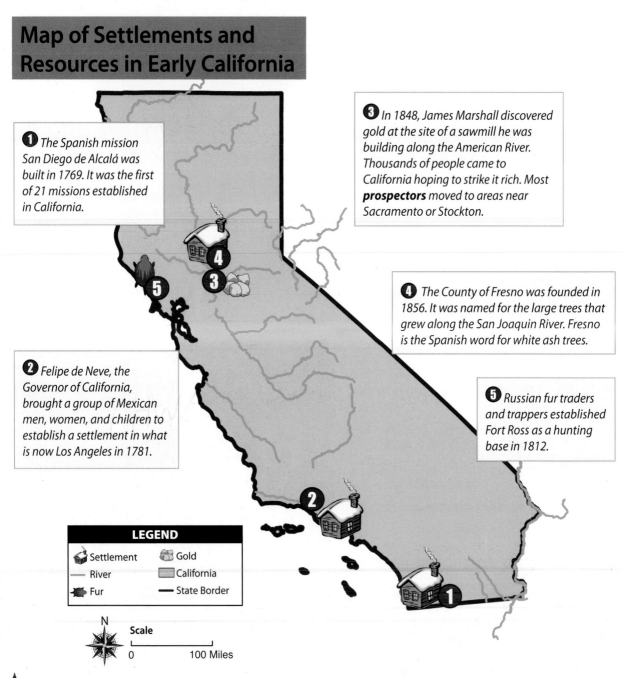

3 In 1848, James Marshall discovered gold at the site of a sawmill he was building along the American River. Thousands of people came to California hoping to strike it rich. Most **prospectors** moved to areas near Sacramento or Stockton.

1 The Spanish mission San Diego de Alcalá was built in 1769. It was the first of 21 missions established in California.

4 The County of Fresno was founded in 1856. It was named for the large trees that grew along the San Joaquin River. Fresno is the Spanish word for white ash trees.

2 Felipe de Neve, the Governor of California, brought a group of Mexican men, women, and children to establish a settlement in what is now Los Angeles in 1781.

5 Russian fur traders and trappers established Fort Ross as a hunting base in 1812.

LEGEND

- 🏠 Settlement
- — River
- 🐢 Fur
- 🟡 Gold
- ⬜ California
- — State Border

N

Scale

0   100 Miles

In 1845 Captain John C. Frémont, an American explorer and soldier, led an expedition to California. At the time war seemed likely between the United States and Mexico because of a dispute over the border of Texas, which had recently become part of the United States. The conflict, known as the Mexican-American War, broke out in April 1846. Less than two months later, in June, American settlers near Sonoma revolted against Mexico and established the California Republic. Frémont supported the settlers and was elected leader of the republic. The republic fell quickly, however, as U.S. forces claimed California for the United States. By the Treaty of Guadalupe Hidalgo, which ended the Mexican-American War in 1848, Mexico gave control of California and the American Southwest to the United States.

More than 260 Americans and many more Mexicans were killed in the Battle of Buena Vista. This Mexican-American War battle was fought on February 23, 1847.

Notable People

Many notable Californians contributed to development of their state and country. Ronald Reagan served as the 33rd governor of California before being elected president in 1980. Steve Jobs, the CEO of Apple Computers, was born in San Francisco and co-founded Apple in what is now Silicon Valley. Aviator Howard Hughes, later played by Leonardo DiCaprio in *The Aviator*, spent most of his life in Los Angeles.

SALLY RIDE (1951–)

Los Angeles–born Sally Ride attended Westlake High School and went on to Stanford University in Palo Alto. In 1978, she beat out 1,000 other applicants for a place in the National Aeronautics and Space Administration (NASA) astronaut program. Ride made history in 1983 when she became the first American woman in space, aboard the space shuttle *Challenger*.

WILLIAM RANDOLPH HEARST (1863–1951)

William Randolph Hearst was born to millionaire parents in San Francisco. While he was attending Harvard University, Hearst's father purchased the *San Francisco Examiner*. Hearst took over the newspaper from his father and then began to acquire papers in other large cities. He later expanded to book publishing and magazines. Today the Hearst Corporation is one of the largest communications companies in the world.

GEORGE PATTON
(1885–1945)

Born in San Gabriel township, George Patton was a United States Army officer who received the prestigious Purple Heart after his service in World War I. He became a household name during World War II after he helped to successfully lead troops in North Africa, Sicily, and France, including in the Battle of the Bulge.

RICHARD M. NIXON
(1913–1994)

Richard Milhous Nixon was a congressman and U.S. senator before being elected president in 1968. He is the only U.S. president born in California, but he is better-known for being the only president ever to resign from office. He resigned after the Watergate scandal, which revealed that Nixon had been involved in covering up illegal activities by members of his staff.

JOHN STEINBECK
(1902–1968)

Born in Salinas, John Steinbeck set many of his novels in California. He received the prestigious Pulitzer Prize for his book *The Grapes of Wrath* and was awarded the Nobel Prize for Literature in 1962. Steinbeck wrote more than twenty-five books in his career, including *East of Eden* and *Of Mice and Men*.

Shirley Temple Black (1928–), one of the most famous child stars in history, left Hollywood to become a U.S. ambassador and diplomat.

Arnold Schwarzenegger (1947–) started his career as a professional bodybuilder, winning the title of "Mr. Universe" when he was 20 years old. After working as an actor in Hollywood for many years, he was elected governor of California in 2003 and served until 2011.

Population

T he majority of California's residents live in urban areas. Much of the population is centered in southern California, particularly from Los Angeles to San Diego. With more than 3.8 million residents, Los Angeles is California's largest city and the second-largest city in the United States, after New York City. San Diego, the second-largest city in California, is home to more than 1.3 million people. Other major cities include Fresno, Long Beach, Oakland, Sacramento, San Francisco, and San Jose.

California Population 1950–2010

California's population is almost four times as large as it was in 1950. What are some reasons that so many people have moved to California since then?

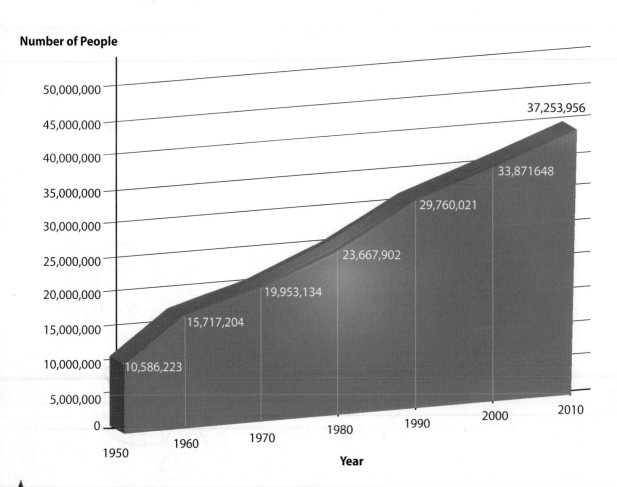

Number of People

50,000,000
45,000,000
40,000,000
35,000,000
30,000,000
25,000,000
20,000,000
15,000,000
10,000,000
5,000,000
0

10,586,223
15,717,204
19,953,134
23,667,902
29,760,021
33,871648
37,253,956

1950
1960
1970
1980
1990
2000
2010

Year

Many of California's Hispanic residents celebrate Mexican Independence day on September 16th.

California's largest county by population is Los Angeles County, which has about 10 million residents.

There are many Buddhist temples throughout California. The architecture and design of these buildings can be very detailed and colorful.

California is home to three of the country's ten most populous cities. They are Los Angeles, San Diego, and San Jose.

California is one of the most ethnically diverse states in the country. The Hispanic population accounts for more than a third of the state's residents. More than one in 10 California residents is of Asian descent, and African Americans make up about 7 percent of the population.

With nearly 4 million residents, Los Angeles is a busy and exciting city.

Politics and Government

California is governed under a state constitution that was adopted in 1879. Like the federal government, California's state government has three branches. The executive branch is headed by a governor, who is responsible for making sure that state laws are carried out. The governor is elected to a four-year term.

Many protests were held at the University of California's Berkeley campus in the 1960s. Students gathered there to voice their disapproval of the Vietnam War.

Before he was elected president, former Hollywood actor Ronald Reagan served as the 33rd governor of California.

Other elected officials of the executive branch include the lieutenant governor, secretary of state, treasurer, attorney general, and controller.

The legislature is composed of a state assembly of 80 members and a state senate of 40 members. The judicial system is headed by the California Supreme Court, which consists of a chief justice and six associate justices. There are many lower courts in the state, which has the largest court system in the United States.

California is divided into 58 counties. Each county has its own elected board of supervisors. The counties usually have a sheriff, district attorney, and county clerk.

I DIDN'T KNOW THAT!

California's state song is called "I Love You California."

Here is an excerpt from the song:

I love you, California, you're the greatest state of all.
I love you in the winter, summer, spring and in the fall.
I love your fertile valleys; your dear mountains I adore.
I love your grand old ocean and I love her rugged shore.
I love your redwood forests—love your fields of yellow grain,
I love your summer breezes, and I love your winter rain,
I love you, land of flowers; land of honey, fruit and wine,
I love you, California; you have won this heart of mine.

Cultural Groups

Many different cultural groups live and work in California. Hispanic Americans, most of whom speak both English and Spanish, make up a large portion of the state's population. Their cultural influence, including foods from Mexico and Central America, can be found throughout the state. A large number of California cities have Spanish names, reflecting the importance of Spanish and Mexican influences. People of Mexican origin celebrate the Mexican holiday called Cinco de Mayo, which means May 5, with festive dancing, music, and feasting. More new immigrants settle in California than in any other state.

California is home to many American Indians.

The San Francisco Chinese New Year celebration features a parade through the city.

Old Town San Diego State Historic Park preserves Mexican and early American buildings built between 1821 and 1872. Mexican culture thrives in this area.

California has the largest number of Spanish-speaking people of any state in the country.

Japanese gardens can be found in several California cities.

San Francisco has one of the largest Chinese American populations of any city in the country. Each year in late January or early February, Chinese New Year is celebrated with the Golden Dragon parade and fireworks. San Francisco's Chinese New Year originated in the 1860s and today is considered the largest Asian event in North America.

California is home to the largest African American population in the western United States, though fewer African Americans live in the West than in other regions of the country. Many African Americans moved to the state during World War II to find work, and their culture is strongly felt throughout the state.

Arts and Entertainment

California's involvement in the motion-picture industry, which is today based in Hollywood, began in the early 1900s. Silent movies were made in the 1920s with actors such as Charlie Chaplin, Laurel and Hardy, and Mary Pickford. In 1927 Walt Disney and his business partner, Ub Iwerks, created a mischievous mouse named Mickey. A short film with sound and music, *Steamboat Willie*, starred Mickey Mouse, with Disney himself providing the voice. Decades of popular films followed, and today the Walt Disney Company is one of the world's leading entertainment corporations.

California is a major center for the performing arts. It has many symphony orchestras, opera companies, and popular musicians. In the 1960s the Beach Boys and other groups became famous for their music celebrating California's beaches and its surfing culture. Today many large music festivals take place in California, including the Monterey Jazz Festival and the Berkeley Festival.

Walt Disney and his staff created many characters who are still popular today, including Mickey Mouse, Donald Duck, and Goofy.

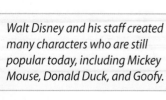

Native Californian Robert Redford has acted in more than forty movies and is also a director.

Actor Leonardo DiCaprio, born in Los Angeles, was kicked off the children's television show *Romper Room* for being "disruptive" when he was 3 years old.

Founded in 1885, Sacramento's Crocker Art Museum is the oldest operating art museum in the western United States.

The famous Hollywood Bowl, a natural amphitheater, has been used since 1922 for summertime concerts under the stars.

Actress Marilyn Monroe was born in Los Angeles. She starred in several major films in the 1950s.

The first film studio in Hollywood was opened on Sunset Boulevard in 1911. Soon after, about 20 companies began producing films, drawn by the warm climate and open spaces. By 1915 Hollywood had become the center of the U.S. film industry. One **landmark** of the district is the famous Grauman's Chinese Theatre, which has footprints and handprints of celebrities in its forecourt. Many of the most famous celebrities in the world live in neighboring communities such as Bel Air and Beverly Hills.

California has produced many writers, entertainers, and artists. San Francisco was the birthplace of the novelist Jack London, author of *The Call of the Wild*, and the poet Robert Frost, who won several Pulitzer Prizes. In the 1950s the **Beat movement** began in San Francisco with poets and authors such as Jack Kerouac. Contemporary writer Amy Tan was born in Oakland. Author Alice Walker, best known for her novel *The Color Purple*, moved to northern California in the late 1970s. Academy Award-winning actor Robert Redford, born in Santa Monica, founded the Sundance Film Festival in 1978.

Sports

California's warm climate and beautiful beaches help make swimming, sailing, and beach volleyball popular. Deep-sea diving allows people to view life in the ocean. California also has excellent locations for surfing and windsurfing. Because of California's climate, many outdoor recreational activities can be enjoyed year-round. Golf is particularly popular in the state. California has hundreds of golf courses, including the famous Pebble Beach course. Because of the state's dramatic differences in climate, a person can golf one day and then go skiing in nearby mountains the next.

Tennis star sisters Venus and Serena Williams grew up in Compton.

Candlestick Park, where the San Francisco 49ers play their home games, can hold more than 70,000 people.

Led by star pitcher Tim Lincecum, the San Francisco Giants won baseball's World Series in 2010. It was their first Series win since the team moved from New York after the 1957 season.

Los Angeles is the largest metropolitan area in the country without a team in the National Football League.

Legendary baseball player Joe DiMaggio is known for playing with the New York Yankees, but he was born in Martinez and spent his childhood in San Francisco.

California has hosted the Summer Olympic Games twice, in 1932 and 1984. It hosted the Winter Olympic Games in 1960.

California has far more professional sports teams than any other state. The state has three teams in the National Football League, five in Major League Baseball, four in the National Basketball Association, and three in the National Hockey League. There are also professional teams in soccer and women's basketball. The San Francisco 49ers football team was the first major league professional sports team in California. The Oakland Raiders and San Diego Chargers football teams have fans throughout the country. Basketball fans flock to see Los Angeles Lakers stars such as Kobe Bryant play at the Staples Center.

National Averages Comparison

The United States is a federal republic, consisting of fifty states and the District of Columbia. Alaska and Hawai'i are the only non-contiguous, or non-touching, states in the nation. Today, the United States of America is the third-largest country in the world in population. The United States Census Bureau takes a census, or count of all the people, every ten years. It also regularly collects other kinds of data about the population and the economy. How does California compare to the national average?

Comparison Chart

United States 2010 Census Data *	USA	California
Admission to Union	NA	September 9, 1850
Land Area (in square miles)	3,537,438.44	155,959.34
Population Total	308,745,538	37,253,956
Population Density (people per square mile)	87.28	238.87
Population Percentage Change (April 1, 2000, to April 1, 2010)	9.7%	10.0%
White Persons (percent)	72.4%	57.6%
Black Persons (percent)	12.6%	6.2%
American Indian and Alaska Native Persons (percent)	0.9%	1.0%
Asian Persons (percent)	4.8%	13.0%
Native Hawaiian and Other Pacific Islander Persons (percent)	0.2%	0.4%
Some Other Race (percent)	6.2%	17.0%
Persons Reporting Two or More Races (percent)	2.9%	4.9%
Persons of Hispanic or Latino Origin (percent)	16.3%	37.6%
Not of Hispanic or Latino Origin (percent)	83.7%	62.4%
Median Household Income	$52,029	$61,017
Percentage of People Age 25 or Over Who Have Graduated from High School	80.4%	76.8%

*All figures are based on the 2010 United States Census, with the exception of the last two items. Percentages may not add to 100 because of rounding.

How to Improve My Community

Strong communities make strong states. Think about what features are important in your community. What do you value? Education? Health? Forests? Safety? Beautiful spaces? Government works to help citizens create ideal living conditions that are fair to all by providing services in communities. Consider what changes you could make in your community. How would they improve your state as a whole? Using this concept web as a guide, write a report that outlines the features you think are most important in your community and what improvements could be made. A strong state needs strong communities.

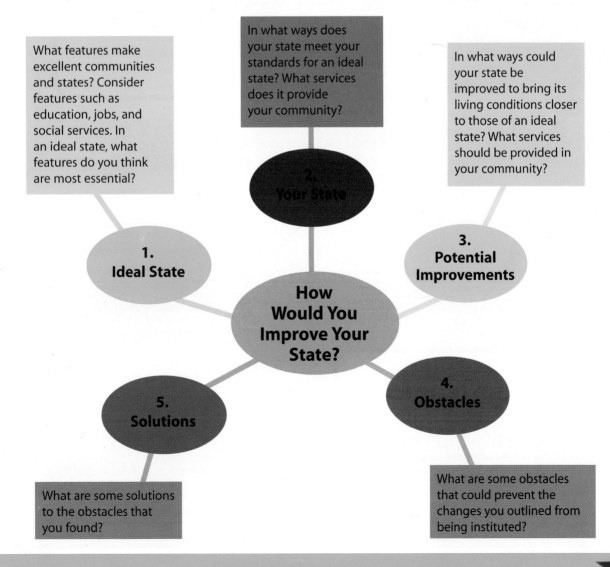

What features make excellent communities and states? Consider features such as education, jobs, and social services. In an ideal state, what features do you think are most essential?

In what ways does your state meet your standards for an ideal state? What services does it provide your community?

In what ways could your state be improved to bring its living conditions closer to those of an ideal state? What services should be provided in your community?

2.
Your State

1.
Ideal State

3.
Potential Improvements

How Would You Improve Your State?

5.
Solutions

4.
Obstacles

What are some solutions to the obstacles that you found?

What are some obstacles that could prevent the changes you outlined from being instituted?

Exercise Your Mind!

Think about these questions and then use your research skills to find the answers and learn more fascinating facts about California. A teacher, librarian, or parent may be able to help you locate the best sources to use in your research.

1 Which trees are the thickest and the tallest in the world?

2 Why was the Golden Gate Bridge painted orange?

3 In what year did Disneyland open?

4 Put the following cities in order from north to south:

Los Angeles   San Francisco
Sacramento   San Diego
Santa Barbara   San Jose

5 What fault causes many of California's earthquakes?

6 In what California city was the first McDonald's restaurant opened?

7 What California zip code has been used in two popular television series?

8 What is the Mother Lode in California?

Words to Know

Beat movement: a social and literary movement in the 1950s that focused on mysticism and relaxed social inhibitions

captivity: the state of being confined, rather than existing in the wild

conservation: protection of the environment

dialects: regional versions of a language

diverse: made up of many different qualities or elements

endangered: in danger of dying out

expedition: a long trip, usually to explore

habitat: the place where a plant or animal lives

hydroelectricity: water-generated power

landmark: a place of historical or cultural importance

missionaries: people sent to another country to do charitable work and convert others to their religion

prospectors: people searching a region for gold or other valuable minerals

quarries: large areas from which stone is obtained

succulents: fleshy plants that are found in desert areas and that can store water in their leaves

Index

Log on to www.av2books.com

AV² by Weigl brings you media enhanced books that support active learning. Go to www.av2books.com, and enter the special code found on page 2 of this book. You will gain access to enriched and enhanced content that supplements and complements this book. Content includes video, audio, web links, quizzes, a slide show, and activities.

Audio
Listen to sections of the book read aloud.

Video
Watch informative video clips.

Embedded Weblinks
Gain additional information for research.

Try This!
Complete activities and hands-on experiments.

WHAT'S ONLINE?

Try This!	**Embedded Weblinks**	**Video**	**EXTRA FEATURES**
Test your knowledge of the state in a mapping activity.	Discover more attractions in California.	Watch a video introduction to California.	**Audio** Listen to sections of the book read aloud.
Find out more about precipitation in your city.	Learn more about the history of the state.	Watch a video about the features of the state.	
Plan what attractions you would like to visit in the state.	Learn the full lyrics of the state song.		**Key Words** Study vocabulary, and complete a matching word activity.
Learn more about the early natural resources of the state.			
Write a biography about a notable resident of California.			**Slide Show** View images and captions, and prepare a presentation.
Complete an educational census activity.			**Quizzes** Test your knowledge.

AV² was built to bridge the gap between print and digital. We encourage you to tell us what you like and what you want to see in the future.

Sign up to be an AV² Ambassador at www.av2books.com/ambassador.